The Greenwich Guide

Day and Night

Graham Dolan

Royal Observatory Greenwich

www.heinemann.co.uk
Visit our website to find out more information about Heinemann Library books.

To order:
 Phone 44 (0) 1865 888066
Send a fax to 44 (0) 1865 314091
Visit the Heinemann Bookshop at www.heinemann.co.uk to browse our catalogue and order online.

First published in Great Britain by Heinemann Library, Halley Court, Jordan Hill, Oxford OX2 8EJ, a division of Reed Educational and Professional Publishing Ltd. Heinemann is a registered trademark of Reed Educational & Professional Publishing Ltd.

OXFORD MELBOURNE AUCKLAND JOHANNESBURG BLANTYRE
GABORONE IBADAN PORTSMOUTH (NH) USA CHICAGO

Designed by Celia Floyd
Illustrations by Jeff Edwards
Originated by Dot Gradations, UK
Printed in Hong Kong/China

05 04 03 02 01
10 9 8 7 6 5 4 3 2 1
ISBN 0 431 13000 0

British Library Cataloguing in Publication Data

Dolan, Graham
  The Greenwich guide to day and night
  1. Time – Juvenile literature   2. Chronology – Juvenile literature
  I. Title   II. Day and night
  529

Acknowledgements
The Publishers would like to thank the following for permission to reproduce photographs:
Pg.4 Francisco Diego; Pg.6 Francisco Diego; Pg.7 Francisco Diego; Pg.11 NHPA; Pg.13 Corbis; Pg.16 National Maritime Museum; Pg.17 National Maritime Museum; Pg.18 Francisco Diego; Pg.19 Francisco Diego; Pg.21 Francisco Diego; Pg.22 National Maritime Museum; Pg.23 [top] Francisco Diego [bottom] National Maritime Museum; Pg.26 National Maritime Museum; Pg.27 [top & bottom] Francisco Diego; Pg.28 Francisco Diego; Pg.29 Francisco Diego.

Cover photograph reproduced with permission of Science Photo Library.

Spine logo reproduced with permission of the National Maritime Museum.

Every effort has been made to contact copyright holders of any material reproduced in this book. Any omissions will be rectified in subsequent printings if notice is given to the Publisher.

Contents

Day and night 4

The Sun 6

The Sun's path across the sky 8

Day and night in different places 10

Shadows 12

Time zones 14

am and pm 16

The sky at night 18

Seasonal stars 20

Our Moon 22

Moon phases 24

Eclipses 26

Factfile 28

Glossary 30

Index 32

Any words appearing in the text in bold, **like this**, are explained in the Glossary.

Day and night

The Sun is our nearest star. We can measure its size and its distance from us. We can see it, but can't touch it, or hear it. It gives us **energy**. Without it, life on Earth would not exist.

During the **day**, we receive light and heat from the Sun. This is when most people eat, drink, work and play. At night, when it is dark, most of us go to bed and sleep. On clear nights, we can see stars and sometimes the Moon and **planets** too.

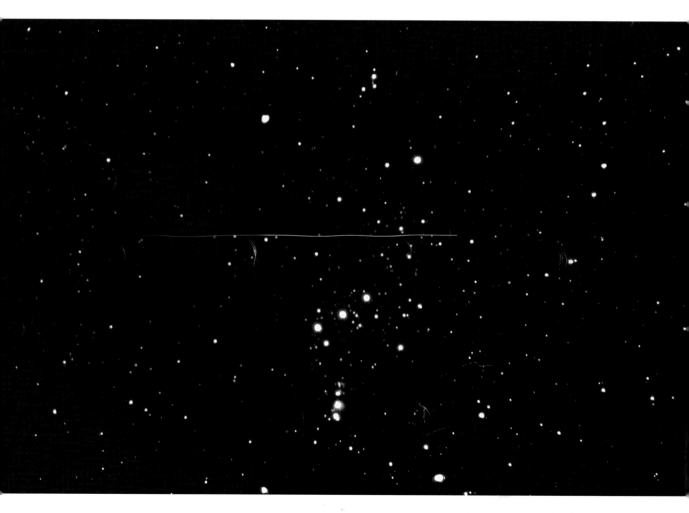

The stars and planets become visible at night.

Our spinning Earth

Our Earth is spinning on its **axis**. Half the Earth always points towards the Sun and half always points away. When the part of the Earth we are on faces the Sun we receive light and energy and we call it **daytime**. As the Earth spins, we eventually end up facing away from the Sun. When this happens, light and energy from the Sun can no longer reach us. It goes dark and **night-time** begins.

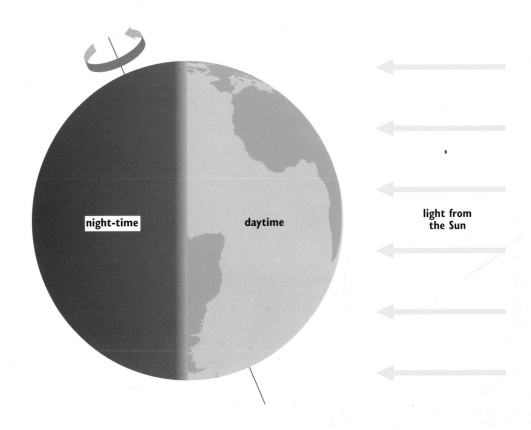

night-time

daytime

light from the Sun

The Earth spins on its axis once each day. The half facing the Sun is in daylight. The half facing away is in darkness.

The Sun

The Sun is just one of thousands of millions of stars that make up our **galaxy**, the Milky Way. It emits light and **energy** which **radiate** out into space. The light and energy travels towards us at 300,000 kilometres (186,000 miles) a second. Travelling at this speed, it takes just over eight minutes to reach the Earth's surface. The next closest star is Proxima Centauri, which is about 250,000 times further away.

The temperature of the Sun

The Sun is a bit like a giant nuclear power station. It produces huge amounts of energy every second. The inside is hotter than the outside. The **temperature** at its centre is about 15 million degrees Celsius. The temperature on the surface is about 5500 degrees Celsius. Dark patches, called sunspots, are sometimes visible. They are regions of the Sun's surface which are cooler than the rest.

The Sun. Never look directly at the Sun! It will damage your eyes. The dark spots are sunspots – each is larger than the Earth.

The Sun's brightness prevents us from seeing other stars during the day.

The size of the Sun

The Sun is about 100 times wider than the Earth and 400 times wider than the Moon. From the Earth, the Sun and the Moon look about the same size in the sky. This is because as well as being 400 times wider than the Moon, the Sun is also about 400 times further away. The actual distance from the Earth to the Sun is about 150 million kilometres (93 million miles).

The Sun's path across the sky

The Sun, Moon and the stars appear to move across the sky in a curve. This is because the Earth is spinning on its **axis**.

The Sun's highest point

The Sun always rises over the **horizon** in the eastern half of the sky, and sets in the western half. It reaches its highest point at **midday**. It rises higher in the summer than it does in the winter. It rises and sets at a slightly different time, and in a slightly different direction, from one **day** to the next.

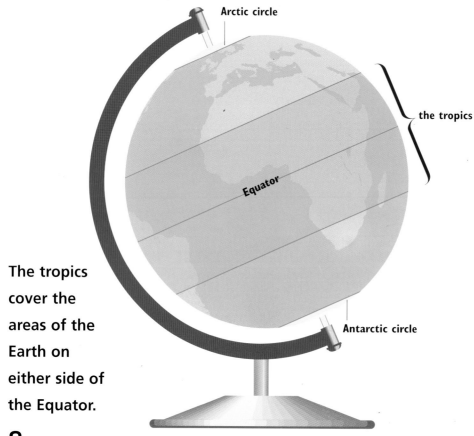

Arctic circle

the tropics

Equator

Antarctic circle

The tropics cover the areas of the Earth on either side of the Equator.

8

Clockwise or anticlockwise?

North of the **tropics**, the midday Sun is always in the south. The Sun appears to move in a **clockwise** direction – from left to right.

South of the tropics, the midday Sun is always in the north. The sun appears to move in an **anticlockwise** direction – from right to left.

In the tropics themselves, the midday sun is sometimes in the north, and sometimes in the south, depending on the time of **year**.

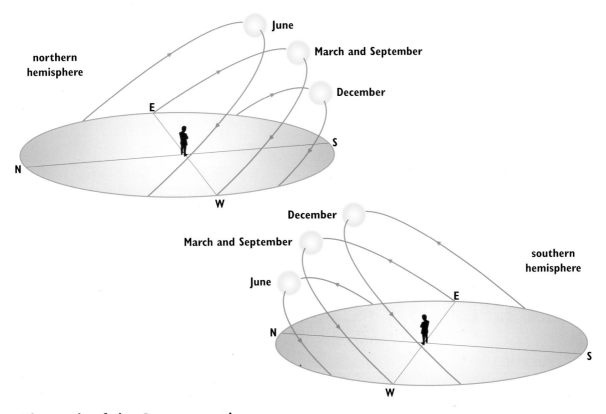

The path of the Sun across the sky at different times of the year.

Day and night in different places

In the summer, there are more hours of daylight each **day** than there are in the winter. This is because the Earth leans as it **orbits** the Sun. In June, the North Pole leans towards the Sun. In December, it leans away from the Sun.

The poles – the land of the midnight Sun

In June, places near the North Pole have 24 hours of daylight each day. In December, they have 24 hours of darkness. Near the South Pole, there are 24 hours of daylight each day in December and 24 hours of darkness in June.

In December, the North Pole points away from the Sun.

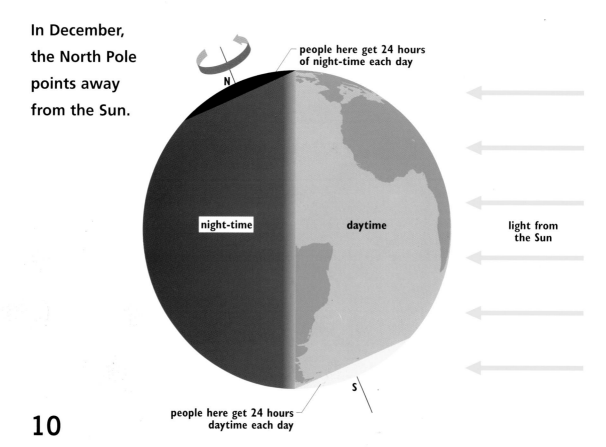

people here get 24 hours of night-time each day

N

night-time

daytime

light from the Sun

S

people here get 24 hours daytime each day

The Equator

Places on the **Equator** get almost equal amounts of **daytime** and **night-time** every day of the **year**. The further north or south of the Equator you go, the greater the difference between the amount of daytime you get each day in the summer and the winter.

The path of the Sun during a summer day near the North Pole.

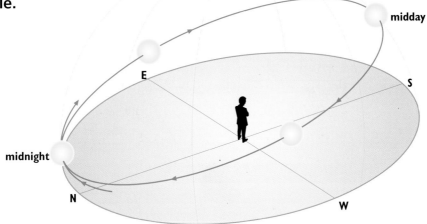

midday

E

S

midnight

N

W

A time-lapse photo shows how around midsummer the Sun in the Polar regions reaches its lowest point at midnight, but does not actually set.

Shadows

When it's sunny, shadows are formed. Shadows can be used to work out the time. They change in length and direction during the **day**.

Length and direction

The length of our shadows depends on the position of the Sun in the sky. As the Sun rises in the sky, the shadows get shorter and shorter. By **midday**, when the Sun is at its highest point, the shadows are at their shortest for that particular day. They then start to get longer again. They grow in length all the time until the Sun sets. The shadows always move in the same **clockwise** or **anticlockwise** direction as the Sun. The shadows at midday always fall along a north–south line.

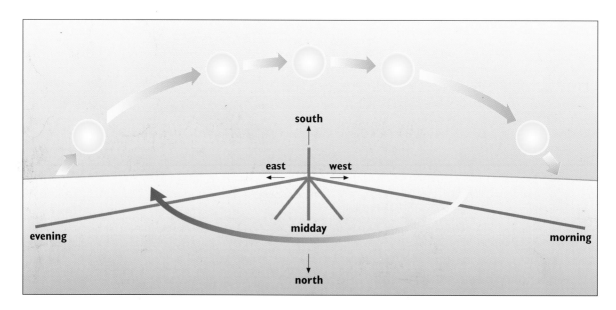

In Europe and the USA, the Sun and shadows moves in a clockwise direction. The midday Sun is always in the south. The midday shadow always points towards the north.

Shadow sticks and sundials

Shadow sticks can be used to follow the path of the Sun across the sky. The shadow of a vertical stick is marked every half-hour with the help of a watch. Although the shadow of the stick always falls in a north–south direction at midday, the exact direction of the other shadows is different at different times of year. As a result, shadow clocks made like this are not a very reliable way of finding out what the time is.

Sundials show the time more accurately. This is because the part that makes the shadow is specially angled. It is called a **gnomon**.

A sundial. The time shown is about 3.30pm.

gnomon

Time zones

Local time

The further west you are, the later the Sun rises, and the later it sets. When a **sundial** in London says 12.00, one in Cardiff to the west will only say 11.48. The time shown by a sundial is called the **local time**. Until about 150 **years** ago, people usually set their clocks and watches using a sundial. Their watches showed the local time. Nowadays, everybody in a particular country or time zone sets their clocks and watches to the same time.

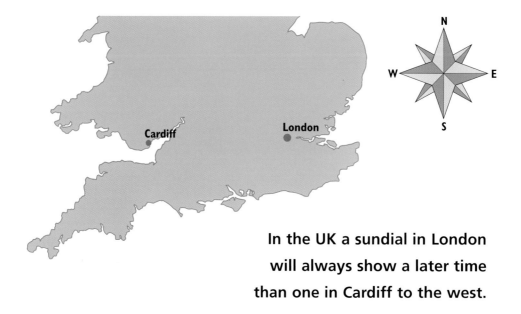

In the UK a sundial in London will always show a later time than one in Cardiff to the west.

Summer time

Some countries use **summer time** for part of the year. Clocks are put forward by an hour in the spring, and put back again in the autumn. The change allows people to make better use of the daylight hours in the summer.

Time zones

The world is divided into **time zones**. The time in each zone is normally one hour different to those on either side. In December, when it is 12.00 noon in London it is 7.00 in the morning in New York, 10.00 in the morning in Rio de Janeiro and 11.00 in the evening in Sydney.

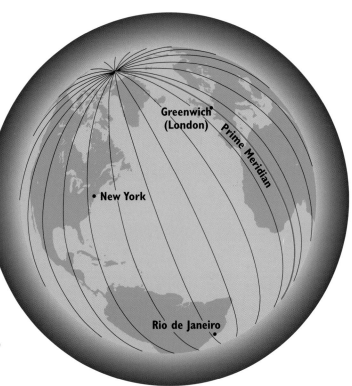

The world's countries fit loosely into a grid of 24 time zones.

Some large countries, such as Australia and the USA, are divided into several time zones. Others, such as China and India, use the same time for the whole country.

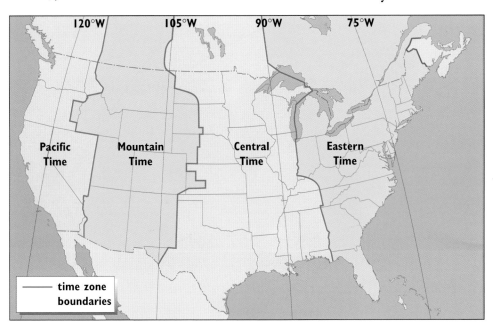

North America's time zones.

15

am and pm

The Sun at midday

At **midday**, the Sun passes from the eastern half of the sky to the western half. The imaginary line dividing the two halves is called a **meridian**. It runs in a north–south direction. When the Sun crosses the meridian, a nearby **sundial** will show 12.00. The Sun will have reached its highest point for the **day** and shadows will be at their shortest.

A sundial says 12.00 when the Sun crosses the meridian at midday.

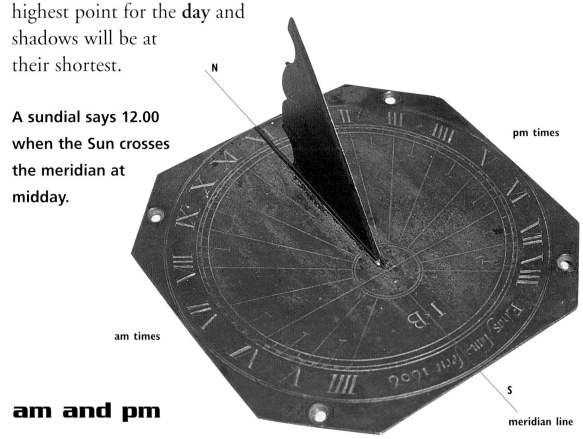

N

pm times

am times

S

meridian line

am and pm

We often use the letters **am** and **pm** when describing time. am stands for the Latin words *ante meridiem*. It means before the Sun has crossed the meridian. pm stands for *post meridiem*. It means after the Sun has crossed the meridian. So 7am is in the morning, but 7pm is in the evening.

Although the Sun will cross the meridian at 12.00 noon according to a sundial, it won't usually do so according to your watch. This is a result of the way in which we set our clocks and watches. The clock time at which the Sun crosses the meridian will depend on your location and the time of year.

A sundial says 12.00 when the Sun reaches its highest point. A watch usually says something different.

Nowadays, we use the words am and pm to mean before and after 12.00. They are no longer directly linked to the Sun's position in the sky.

The sky at night

At night, when the Sun is lighting up the other side of the Earth, we can see some of the millions of other stars.

The constellations

On a clear night in the countryside, it is possible to look up and see about two thousand stars. On some nights, the Moon can be seen as well. In the past, sailors used the Moon and the stars to find their way at sea. The stars move across the sky in curves in a similar way to the Sun. They appear to make patterns in the sky. Some of the patterns look a bit like animals or people. In ancient times, people gave them names. Each pattern is called a **constellation**. The sky is divided into 88 constellations.

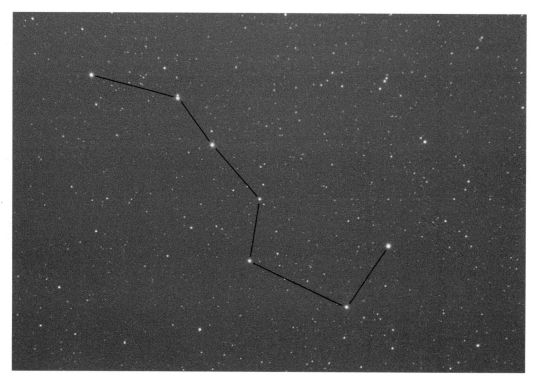

The Plough or Big Dipper is part of the constellation called the Great Bear. It looks a bit like a saucepan in the sky and is one of the easiest groups of stars to recognize.

The planets

As well as the stars, we can sometimes see the **planets** Mercury Venus, Mars, Jupiter and Saturn. Although they look like stars in the sky, they are seen in different constellations as the **months** and **years** go by. Occasionally, two or more planets are seen very close together in the sky.

Venus and Jupiter are brighter than all the stars except the Sun. They can be seen here with Saturn and the Moon.

Seasonal stars

From the **Equator**, you can see all the stars at some point during the **year**. Most of them can be seen at some stage during any particular night. Away from the Equator, some stars can always be seen, some are never visible and some can sometimes be seen.

Circumpolar stars

The stars that can always be seen are called **circumpolar stars**. As the Earth spins on its **axis**, the circumpolar stars in the **northern hemisphere** appear to rotate around the **Pole Star** (Polaris).

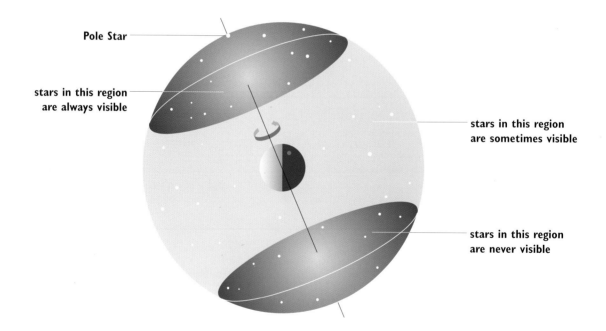

Pole Star

stars in this region are always visible

stars in this region are sometimes visible

stars in this region are never visible

From the Earth, the stars look as though they are fixed to a giant rotating sphere. This diagram shows which stars can be seen from southern England (the red dot) and places in the world at the same distance from the North Pole.

Seeing Orion

The rest of the visible stars can be seen at some times but not at others. This is because they rise and set, like the Sun. Each **day** they rise and set about four minutes earlier than they did the day before. This means that for part of the year they appear in the sky at the same time as the Sun. The **constellation Orion**, for example, is only visible for part of the **year**. At the other times it appears in the sky during our **daytime**. The Sun is so bright that we can't see Orion and the other stars.

Orion the Hunter. This picture was taken in the northern hemisphere. In the **southern hemisphere** Orion appears the other way up.

Our Moon

The Moon is our nearest neighbour in space. It is smaller than the Earth. The Earth is about four times wider. The Moon is covered in craters. They were formed when **meteoroids** – lumps of rock in our **solar system** – collided with the Moon. Most were formed thousands of millions of **years** ago while the Moon was still very young.

Things weigh less on the Moon

On the Moon, you would weigh less than you do on the Earth. The force of **gravity** is less because the Moon is smaller. There isn't enough gravity for the Moon to be able to hang on to an atmosphere.

The Moon rises and sets like the Sun. In this picture, it is about to set.

The surface of the Moon is covered in craters.

The far side of the Moon

The Moon turns on its **axis** once every 27.3 days. This is exactly the same rate that it **orbits** the Earth. Because of this, the same side of the Moon always faces towards us. Nobody knew what the far side of the Moon looked like until 1959, when pictures were sent back to Earth by a Russian spacecraft. The USA is the only country to have landed people on the Moon. The first time was in July 1969. The sixth and last time was in December 1972.

near side

far side

This model of the Moon was made before anyone knew what the far side of the Moon looked like.

Moon phases

Reflecting light from the Sun

The Moon has no light of its own. We can only see it because it reflects light from the Sun. Half of the Moon always points towards the Sun and half always points away. We are not always able to see the whole of the lit half that faces the Sun. The amount of the lit face that can be seen changes as the Moon **orbits** the Earth. You can see the different **phases of the moon** in the diagram below.

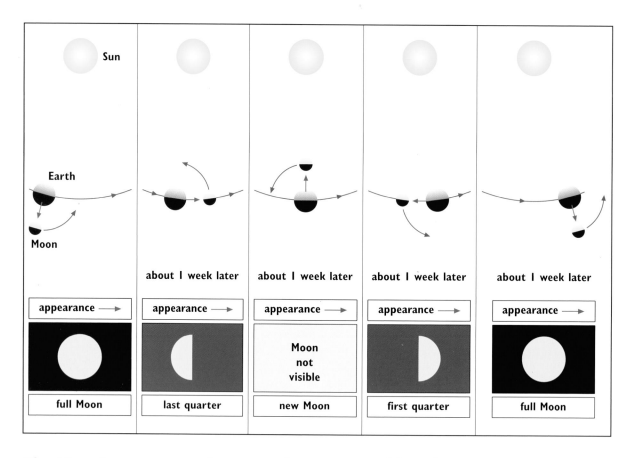

The Moon's appearance changes as it goes around its orbit. In Australia, the Moon appears the opposite way up to how it appears in the UK.

New Moon and full Moon

When the Sun and the Moon are on opposite sides of the Earth, the whole of the lit face can normally be seen. We call this a full Moon. Roughly two weeks later, when the Moon passes between the Earth and the Sun, none of the lit face can be seen. We call this a new Moon.

The Moon from day to night

The Moon rises and sets roughly 50 minutes later from one **day** to the next. This means that on some nights, it will not be visible when it gets dark, but it may be visible when it gets light.

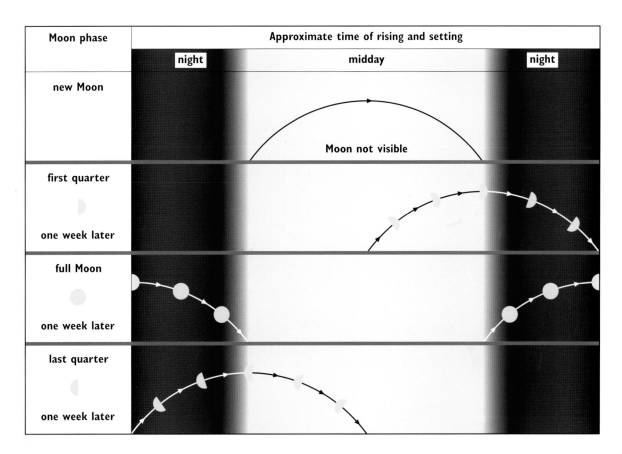

Different phases of the Moon are seen at different times of the day.

Eclipses

Eclipses of the Sun

The Moon goes round the Earth. Every $29\frac{1}{2}$ **days**, it passes between the Sun and the Earth, and there is a new Moon. Normally the Moon doesn't block the Sun from view when this happens. This is because its **orbit** is tilted. It passes unseen above or below the Sun.

A solar **eclipse** occurs if the Moon passes in front of the Sun and blocks part or all of it from view. During a total eclipse, the Moon completely blocks the Sun from view for a few seconds or minutes. When this happens, the **temperature** drops, and it gets dark enough for the street lamps to come on.

Many people use specially-made filters to observe solar eclipses. Never look directly at the Sun! Even using sunglasses it will damage your eyes and could make you go blind.

Eclipses of the Moon

When there is a full Moon, an eclipse of the Moon will sometimes occur. The Moon is on the opposite side of the Earth to the Sun. The Earth gets in the way, and prevents some of the Sun's light from falling on the Moon. In most lunar eclipses, part or all of the bright surface of the Moon goes very dark.

A partial eclipse of the Sun.

A total eclipse of the Sun – the dark circle is the Moon.

Factfile

Not everyone calculates their **days** in the same way. Days in the Jewish and Muslim calendars begin at sunset rather than at midnight.

The last total **eclipse** of the Sun of the last **millennium** occurred on 11 August 1999. It was visible from parts of the UK, central Europe, the Middle East and Asia.

When the Sun is very low in the sky, its shape appears to be oval – an effect caused by the bending of light by the Earth's atmosphere.

It gets dark more suddenly after the Sun has set when you are closer to the **Equator**.

The Moon can only be seen at the time of new moon during an eclipse of the Sun.

Summer time was first suggested by William Willett in 1907. His original idea was to put the clocks forward in four steps of 20 minutes for four weeks in a row.

In the European Union, summer time starts on the last Sunday in March. It ends on the last Sunday in October. In New Zealand and parts of Australia, summer time begins in October and ends in March.

If all the lights in a city were turned off, people living there would be able to see about ten times as many stars in the night sky.

Days and nights used to be shorter. The length of our day has increased by nearly 10% over the last 400 million years as the Earth's spin has slowed down.

As well as radiating light and energy, the Sun also throws particles out into space. When lots of particles arrive from the Sun at once, the night sky flickers with coloured light – an effect known as an aurora.

Glossary

am   originally used to mean a time in the morning before the sun had crossed the meridian. Nowadays it is used to mean a time in the morning before 12.00.

anticlockwise   the opposite direction to the way in which the hands on a clock move

axis   an imaginary line passing from the North to the South Pole through the centre of a planet, around which the planet spins

circumpolar star   a star that is always visible in a clear night sky

clockwise   the direction in which the hands of a clock move

constellation   a group of stars in the night sky

day   a length of time based on the time it takes for the Earth to spin round once on its axis

daytime   the time between sunrise and sunset

eclipse   when the Moon passes in front of the Sun, a solar eclipse occurs. When the Earth prevents the Sun's light from falling on the Moon, a lunar eclipse occurs.

energy   what it takes to heat something up or to make it move

Equator   an imaginary line that separates the Earth's northern and southern hemispheres

galaxy   a group of stars (usually a billion or more) on its own in space

gnomon   the part of a sundial that casts the shadow

gravity   a force that attracts objects to each other. The Earth's gravity gives us our weight.

horizon   the line where the sky appears to meet the Earth

local time   a time system which uses the actual position of the Sun in the sky

meridian   a line that runs in a north-south direction (and if extended would pass through the Earth's North and South Poles)

meteoroid   a rock-like object that is travelling through space

midday   the time when the Sun reaches its highest point of the day (and crosses the meridian)

millennium   a period of 1000 years

month   a lenth of time based on the time it takes for the Moon to orbit the Earth once

night-time   the time between sunset and sunrise

northern hemisphere the half of the Earth north of the Equator – the top half of a globe

orbit the path of a planet around the Sun or a moon around a planet

Orion one of the constellations of stars that can be seen from Earth

phase of the Moon the shape of the lit portion of the Moon as seen from the Earth

planet an object in the shape of a ball that orbits the Sun

Plough part of the constellation the Great Bear

pm originally used to mean a time in the afternoon or evening after the Sun had crossed the meridian, but nowadays used to mean a time in the afternoon or evening after 12.00

Pole Star the star situated directly above the Earth's North Pole – the only star that does not appear to move as the Earth spins on its axis

radiate when energy is sent out in waves or rays

solar system the Sun, together with the planets like Earth that orbit the Sun

southern hemispere the half of the Earth south of the Equator – the bottom half of the globe

summer time the time used in some countries during the summer months. It is normally one hour ahead of the time used during the winter months.

sundial a device that uses shadows to find the time from the Sun's position in the sky

temperature how hot or cold something is

time zone a part of the Earth in which everyone sets their clocks and watches to the same time

tropics the part of the Earth near the Equator

year a length of time based on the time taken for the Earth to orbit the Sun and for the cycle of seasons to repeat itself. A normal calendar year has 365 days. A leap year has 366 days.

Index

am   16
aurora   29
Big Dipper, the   18
calendar
  Jewish   28
  Muslim   28
circumpolar stars   20
clock   14, 17, 29
constellations   18
day   4, 8, 10, 12, 16, 21, 25, 26, 28, 29
daylight   10, 14
daytime   5, 11, 21
Earth, the
  axis   5, 8, 20
  orbit of the Sun   10
  slowing down   29
  spinning   5, 8
energy   4, 5, 6, 29
Equator   11, 20, 28
galaxy   6
gnomon   13
gravity   22
Great Bear, the   18
Jupiter   19
local time   14
Mars   19
meridian   16, 17
meteoroids   22
Milky Way, the   6
millennium   28
Moon   4, 7, 8, 18, 19, 22–27, 28
  axis   23
  eclipse of the Moon   27
  eclipse of the Sun   26, 28
  full Moon   25, 27
  landing on the Moon   23
  new Moon   25, 26, 28
  orbit of the Earth   23, 24, 26
  phases   24, 25

night-time   5, 11
North Pole   10, 20
northern hemisphere   20, 21
Orion   21
planet   4, 19
Plough, the   18
pm   16
Pole Star (Polaris)   20
Proxima Centauri   6
Saturn   19
shadow   12–13, 16
shadow clock   13
shadow stick   13
South Pole   10
southern hemisphere   21
star   4, 6, 8, 18, 20, 21, 29
summer   8, 10, 11, 14
summer time   14, 28, 29
Sun   4, 5, 6, 7, 8, 10, 12, 14, 17, 18, 21, 22,
      24, 25, 27, 28, 29
  eclipse   26, 28
  midnight Sun   10
  path of the Sun   11, 12, 16
sundial   13, 14, 16, 17
sunspot   6
temperature   6, 26
time zone   14–15
tropics   9
Venus   19
watch   13, 14, 17
winter   8, 10, 11
year   14, 19, 20, 21, 22